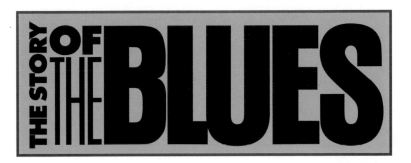

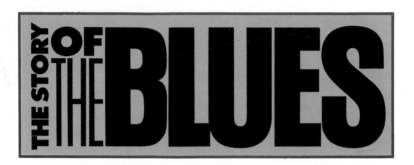

THE STORY OF THE BLUES

Peter O.E. Bekker, Jr.

FRIEDMAN/FAIRFAX
PUBLISHERS

A FRIEDMAN/FAIRFAX BOOK

© 1994, 1997 Michael Friedman Publishing Group, Inc.

Library of Congress Cataloging-In-Publication Data.

Bekker, Peter O. E.
    The story of the blues/Peter O.E. Bekker, Jr.
       p.   cm.
    Discography:
    Includes bibliographical references (p.   ) and index.
    ISBN 1-56799-357-5
    1. Blues (Music)—History and criticism.   I. Title.   II. Series
ML3521.B45   1997
781.643'09—dc20   96-38465
                                                CIP

Editor: Nathaniel Marunas
Art Director: Jeff Batzli
Designer: Lynne Yeamans
Photography Editor: Jennifer Crowe McMichael

Color separations by Ocean Graphic International Company Ltd.
Printed in Singapore by KHL Printing Co. Pte Ltd.

10 9 8 7 6 5 4 3 2 1

For bulk purchases and special sales, please contact:
Friedman/Fairfax Publishers
15 West 26th Street
New York, NY 10010
(212) 685-6610 FAX (212) 685-1307

Visit our website: http://www.metrobooks.com

Acknowledgments

The blues would have gotten around without chroniclers, just as any great and powerful art gets around without them. Still, so much would have been lost if not for the work of those impresarios, academics, and buffs who thought to record and therefore immortalize the early Delta bluesmen and their cousins from around the way. Their motives differed, ranging from the pursuit of profit to the pursuit of knowledge to the pursuit of a Holy Grail. Mostly nameless and faceless these many years later, these devoted men and women are responsible for the preservation of the material on the accompanying disc. In seeking out and recording the music of the early players, the first chroniclers and recordists have incalculably enhanced our understanding of the roots of the Delta blues.

Contents

Introduction

The blues music of the Mississippi Delta has been played and sung since at least the turn of the twentieth century. How long it was played before that is a question that may never be answered. Like spirituals, gospel, and jazz, Delta blues is the music of slaves and former slaves, a group that was thought of as chattel for hundreds of years and whose cultural and artistic progress in the Americas went woefully undocumented.

Only recently have serious attempts been made to untangle the evolution of African-American artistry; the task is daunting. It amounts to a backward search into the mist and haze of an era when the majority of blacks were purposely kept anonymous, illiterate, and isolated by their owners, and later by their "betters." Without reliable documentation, what is known about the roots of African-American music has mostly been inferred. Researchers use the scant resources available, such as early recordings and the personal, but often contradictory, recollections of old musicians and their relatives, friends, and descendants.

Recollections, of course, are fallible. They often lack important detail, and even consistency. Memories grow dim and they are often at odds with hard evidence when that's available. Even the indisputable truth of preserved recordings is a mixed blessing. Quite a few recordings of early Delta blues singers survive, but they raise more questions than they answer. Records were not made until the technology itself was developed late in the nineteenth century. Even then, blacks were not recorded with any regularity until, unexpectedly, vaudeville singer Mamie Smith (1883–1946) recorded a rendition of "Crazy Blues" in 1920 that sold thousands of copies, paving the way for the era of the "race record." Delta blues as it appears on even the earliest recordings is practically fully developed.

Lost is the music of the primogenitors; the contributions they made to the evolution of the blues may never be known.

The academic search for specifics about the roots of the Delta blues is now well under way. It is a search that may clarify and quantify, but it is a search that would probably mystify the ancestors of the early bluesmakers, who, like their descendants, knew that the most important information is to be found in the music itself. Blues music resonates, in apparent simplicity, with the collective voice of people who have endured hundreds of years of slavery and oppression. To understand, one must listen.

Mamie Smith, a determined woman with a powerful singing style, was the first blues singer to have a best-selling record.

Roots

There was no tradition of written history among the West Africans whose tribes were plundered by slave traders (and who sometimes took or sold their relatives and tribe members into slavery because of rivalries and tribal ambitions). Theirs was an oral tradition in which instrumental music, songs, and dances were long established as the main ways to celebrate and memorialize events. This was generally so; slaves, after all, were taken from quite a few tribes that inhabited a huge area of African territory, ranging from what is now Senegal, down along the Atlantic coast to the mouth of the Congo River. Folkways and their expression differed significantly from one group to another, but in most cases each tribe had its cadre of professional singers and storytellers who were living encyclopedias of tribal history and keepers of a comprehensive body of lore. Through their rituals and songs, these tribal "historians" passed along important myths, folkways, and customs from one generation to the next.

Every event of consequence—births, deaths, hunts, feasts, plantings, harvests—was celebrated in song, in which the entire tribe would very often participate. In the westernmost territories now called Senegal and Gambia (and known then to slave traders as Senegambia), whole villages would take part in elaborate rituals involving call-and-response singing; frenzied, complex drumming; and complicated hand-clapping. Those

Living insular and segregated lives, slaves in the Americas were subject to an apartheid rigorously enforced by slave owners, whose sentiment was that blacks were separate and by no means equal.

rituals were usually presided over by members of a social caste, called griots, whose role was to sing and to entertain, but who might also provide constructive accompaniment, for example, to set the pace for farmers and other gangs of workers.

Those traditions came to the Americas with enslaved Africans and were influenced and transformed by the collective experience of hundreds of years of bondage and oppression. More than an outlet for expressions of hopelessness and despair, tribal songs were often written and used as a secret language to plot rebellions and escapes. The ritual of "secret meetings" (also called Brush Arbor or Camp Meetings in the colonies) was another custom imported by slaves to the Americas. In Africa, secret meetings were a way for elders to pass along important tribal customs to younger members, usually at a ritual gathering in an isolated place. In the Americas, slaves also gathered secretly at such meetings, often summoned to them, as their ancestors had been, by the beat of a drum or the blare of a horn.

The meetings gave a sense of community and continuity to people who were completely adrift in foreign surroundings, existing there in servitude. At the meetings, which were segregated by gender and held in the woods or some other remote location unknown to the slave owners, the participants danced and sang, often at fever pitch, for many hours. It was common for them to rage bitterly against their bondage and plan ways of escape (the goal was usually to go back to Africa). The "minutes" of these meetings often emerged as a communal song that could be heard for weeks afterward, plaintively drifting through the slave quarters.

Slave owners had good reason to fear rebellions. Bloody uprisings claimed many lives in several places in the Caribbean and in Central and South America. In addition, in Virginia, seventy-three people died in the 1831 Nat Turner rebellion, an insurgence that had been arranged at secret gatherings. The latter happened despite the ban that had been imposed in 1676 on secret meetings and other "African cult" gatherings (especially those called by the beat of a drum). There was no effective way, however, for slave owners to silence the voices of the enslaved; the will to survive drove those in bondage to express in traditional ways their outlooks on their lives and their dire circumstances. In increasing numbers, music and song were used to channel the determination to obtain freedom—at whatever cost.

Spirituals and Jazz

In North America the expression of these sentiments often took the form of chants and songs in the clipped and imprecise words of people who were taught only enough English to allow them to function as slaves. As they had in Africa, the songs sometimes described mundane events, but at other times, the songs were made up of words (created either extemporaneously or learned from Protestant hymnals, and embellished with "moaning" bluesy vocalizations) that poignantly expressed the rage, pain, and hopelessness of their life of enslavement. These were the chants and songs that came to be known as spirituals, and they probably emerged concurrently with the first music that would later be called the blues.

The earliest spirituals, or slave songs, are filled with Christian sentiments that were often not at all heartfelt. Christianity was not widespread among slaves before the mid-1800s. It had been introduced earlier by nervous owners, mostly in hopes of pacifying the growing unrest in their slave pens. In fact, biblical references usually had a different meaning to the blacks who sang spirituals. To these singers, "Canaan," "Heaven," and other synonyms for "The Promised Land" were encoded references to Africa, or some other place of freedom; "God," "Lord," "Moses," and other biblical figures probably represented people or concepts of significance to the community in the particular place and time the spiritual was created.

Christianity was eventually sincerely embraced by many enslaved blacks. Following Emancipation, spirituals evolved into jubilees, which were performed in formal concerts by trained singers, usually students attending all-black colleges (these began to open at the end of the Civil War). The Fisk Jubilee

The 1873 Fisk Jubilee Singers made a triumphant tour of Europe appearing before Queen Victoria and other notables. The proceeds paid for Jubilee Hall on the Fisk campus, the first permanent structure in the United States dedicated to the education of blacks.

Singers are credited with popularizing spirituals as a popular concert form. The fate of the Fisk School in Nashville hung in the balance when they embarked on a fund-raising tour of the Midwest and East Coast in 1871. Their program, mostly traditional European choral music, was getting only polite responses from audiences. Then, spontaneously, the decision was made in Ohio to end a concert for a convention of Congregational ministers with some spirituals. The reaction was so enthusiastic that the Fisk Singers began performing spirituals exclusively, creating

a craze among other black schools, which quickly began doing the same. Jubilees also became popular among impromptu quartets or quintets, amateurs from a particular neighborhood who enjoyed getting together to sing. It was only a short evolutionary step from those neighborhood jubilee groups to the long line of such tremendously successful professional ensembles as the Ink Spots, the Mills Brothers, the Ravens, the Five Satins, and Smokey Robinson and the Imperials.

"Classic" Blues and Gospel

By the turn of the century quite a lot was happening among black musicians. Jazz was taking shape in several southern cities, primarily New Orleans. Black instrumentalists were experimenting with an informal mishmash of folk music, popular tunes, and European classical music. W.C. Handy (1873–1958) had already heard blues being played during a trip through the Mississippi Delta. Soon after, he wrote two of his most famous pieces, "Memphis Blues" and "St. Louis Blues," neither of which, it is certain, bore any resemblance to the music

Bessie Smith (1898–1937)

Starting with girlhood street corner appearances in the ramshackle Chattanooga, Tennessee, neighborhood in which she was born, Bessie Smith was a trouper all her life. By the time of her death, Bessie Smith was known around the world. She was a beloved diva who appeared with the best players of the day at sold-out concerts in theaters coast to coast. Smith's pleasing contralto and mesmerizing showmanship propelled her from poverty to international fame as a singer of "classic" blues tunes, many of which she wrote or cowrote. Before the Great Depression, Smith was the highest-paid black entertainer in the world, collecting as much as two thousand dollars a week to sing such songs as her own "Nobody Knows You When You're Down and Out," "Empty Bed Blues," and "Backwater Blues," accompanied by the finest musicians of the day, including Louis Armstrong, Lonnie Johnson, and Benny Goodman.

Smith joined minstrel and vaudeville troupes in her teens, including a 1913 stint with the Rabbit Foot Minstrels that brought her together with blues legend Gertrude "Ma" Rainey, who no doubt influenced the younger woman's showmanship, if not her singing style. Smith's elegant contralto and her hypnotizing delivery differs dramatically from that of Rainey, who very often sang hard-edged numbers in a rough, barrelhouse style. Because of her early stage experience, Smith's repertoire was extensive by the time she made her first record in 1923. Possibly because of her association with "Ma" Rainey, Smith specialized in blues numbers, singing more by far than any other female vocalist of the day. She also performed country blues, vaudeville, and jazz tunes in a show that completely captivated her audiences.

"Downhearted Blues" (b/w "Gulf Coast Blues") was an immediate hit when it was released in 1923, setting Smith well on the way to international fame, although she had to struggle to sustain her career during the Great Depression. Bessie Smith, the "Empress of the Blues," died in a tragic 1937 car accident in Mississippi.

he had heard in Mississippi. Like most of Handy's "blues," those two compositions had much more in common with popular ragtime tunes of the day, from which Handy would frequently "borrow" material. But it was from the pirated music of composers like Handy that "classic" blues would blossom. It soon became a very popular and comparatively sophisticated ensemble-based music, with lyrics sung compellingly by monumental talents such as Gertrude "Ma" Rainey (1886–1939), Bessie Smith, Ida Cox (1898–1967), and the legendary Billie Holiday (1915–1959).

In the early 1900s, the jubilee began to evolve into a sacred music that was joyfully optimistic with none of the anguished and lonely laments that had characterized slave songs. The new music was called gospel and it exploded from black churches, revival tents, and tenements, spurred by the Pentecostal resurgence that swept the nation at the turn of the century. Although gospel was the stepchild of blues and jazz, its adherents were not at all sympathetic to the prodigal and profligate practitioners of the older forms. Nor would they be especially forgiving of the lambs, such as Ray Charles (b. 1930) and Aretha Franklin (b. 1942), who would later abandon the flock to pursue and popularize a new, secular music; in the 1950s and 1960s, these lost lambs contributed to the growth of a dynamic hybrid called soul.

Of particular interest during the early twentieth century is the spread of the music that W.C. Handy, an educated man and a trained musician, apparently failed to appreciate. He certainly wouldn't be the last. The blues that was beginning to surface in the dusty expanse of the Mississippi Delta was a primal, guttural, sexual, and even frightening music. It was

A sophisticated ragtime player and dance-band leader, W.C. Handy dismissed Delta blues as "primitive" when he first heard it around the turn of the century.

often the purview of dangerous men living in a dangerous land. Its rhythms and tempos were harsh and insistent, and its overall message was often subtle, although the music spoke so directly of love, lust, betrayal, and misfortune that some people found it threatening. Indeed, rock and roll, the most famous offspring of the blues—itself considered by many to be satanic—would also be considered "the Devil's music" one day. The music that W.C. Handy had overlooked was the daddy of electrified Chicago blues and the granddaddy of rock and roll.

King Cotton

White penetration into the swamps and forests of northwestern Mississippi began in earnest after 1820, when the Choctaw Indians began ceding land to the U.S. government, which could be quite persuasive (to say the least) in such matters. Although the mouth of the Mississippi River lay hundreds of miles to the south, settlers began calling this fertile expanse of bottomland, bordered on the north by Memphis and on the

south by Vicksburg, the Delta. Straddling the great river that nurtures the region, the natural topography dictates the Delta's western and eastern boundaries, which stretch from the lowlands of eastern Arkansas across to the low hills of central Mississippi.

Planters knew that with its forests cleared and swamps drained, the Delta would be a vast, flat, spectacularly fertile plain, ideal for growing cotton. So it was into that semi-tamed area that pioneering southerners, mostly prosperous planters, brought their households and slaves and began carving out and tending to the vast cotton fields that would help fuel the ravenous demands of a prosperous South and an industrializing world.

The Civil War, of course, derailed the South's agricultural juggernaut. By the end of the war there was no more Confederacy, and the economy of the southern United States was shattered. The defeat brought profound change that eventually reunited a nation, but only grudgingly, haltingly, incrementally. Blacks benefited from the social adjustments that had accompanied the South's defeat, but only during the earliest days of Reconstruction. Emancipation from slavery was at the top of the list of improvements, a list that also included free public education and the elimination of racially discriminatory laws. But the many promises of the early postwar years were not kept. Windows of opportunity, never opened completely for blacks, were slammed shut almost immediately with the onset in the late 1800s of "Jim Crow" laws. Named for a mocking minstrel-show caricature, these laws promoted and justified a "separate but equal" caste system in most southern states, a system officially sanctioned in 1896 by the Supreme Court's decision in *Plessy* v. *Ferguson*.

It was during that period of bitter white recrimination, social backsliding, and racial violence that blacks began an enormous migration to the urban centers of the North. For those who remained, life changed very little; many blacks stayed on the plantations that had either been abandoned or sold by their destitute owners. No longer slaves, neither were they employed. Most had to scramble just to survive.

The answer to the needs of both destitute planters and destitute former slaves was the sharecropper system. It evolved as the only quick option to salvage the South's agrarian economy. Blacks who agreed to stay on plantations to sow, pick, and chop cotton were promised a share of the proceeds at harvest time. The system worked well on paper, but in practice many blacks never seemed to make out. In some cases, because planters deducted the cost of food, clothing, and housing from an already meager wage, the sharecropper would end the year in debt. The debt would be carried over to the next year, and the next, until the sharecropper was again living in servitude, this time virtual if not actual. Of course, there was nothing to prevent the sharecropper from leaving the plantation and his debts behind. There was plenty of movement in the Delta, with "hands" traveling from one plantation to another seeking better jobs or simply reveling in the freedom of travel for its own sake—a heady experience for a former slave. A few of the travelers carried guitars, and it was usually they who carried the Delta blues.

Charley Patton

A minstrel much more than a pure blues-man, Charley Patton (1887–1934) performed in many styles, for many constituencies, and under many circumstances in his years of rambling throughout the Mississippi Delta. Unlike the legacies of most of his contemporaries who also helped shape the Delta blues during the early part of the twentieth century, Patton's legacy as a powerful singer and blues pioneer is forever unassailable because of the recordings he made for Paramount Records, many of which were commercially successful in their time. The excellence of those sides and the lingering presence of their essence in the music of his peers and of later blues players make Patton one of the most important practitioners of the form. Not that everything he sang or recorded was original—blues, like any folk music, was passed along from player to player and reflected many of their styles and personalities. Verses floated around and were liberally borrowed and exchanged. The same was so for the music. But simply by using and adding to it, innovators like Patton shaped and nurtured a music that at the turn of the century was by no means strictly defined. His was a generation whose very personal input gave form and substance to the Delta blues; furthermore, their contributions can be heard as recognizable elements in the work of countless subsequent players.

The anecdotes and recollections of friends, acquaintances, and family members summarize Charley Patton as a physically small man—wiry, blustery, probably high-strung—who rarely missed an opportunity to have a good time. He had a surprisingly gruff singing voice for a man of his small size, and he accompanied himself on guitar in an equally gritty style.

Born on a farm outside the community of Edwards in Hinds County, Mississippi, Patton was raised a little further north, in the Delta, on the Will Dockery plantation near Cleveland, in Sunflower County, Mississippi—forty square miles on which, some say, the Delta blues was born. Quite a few musicians whose names are now famous spent time on Dockery's, all of them to listen to and learn from Charley Patton: Willie Brown, Howlin' Wolf (1910–1976), and Roebuck Staples

(b. 1915), whose family performs today as the Staples Singers, to name just a few. Other now legendary contemporaries who acknowledged their debt to Patton include Eddie "Son" House, with whom Patton played and recorded; Robert Johnson, now called by some "King of the Delta Blues"; Muddy Waters, who went on to define the style called Chicago blues; Booker T. Washington "Bukka" White; and, by extension, just about every blues player in succeeding generations.

Patton, his eleven brothers and sisters, his father Bill, and his mother Anne performed the usual backbreaking and menial chores on Will Dockery's cotton plantation. Charley was a field hand and a mule driver until, in his early twenties, he was fired by a foreman for reasons that are not clear. It was then, in the first decade of the twentieth century, that Patton began his rambles throughout Mississippi and as far afield as Wisconsin and New York City, taking with him at the outset his guitar and the religious songs he had learned (the latter to placate his father, who was an elder in a plantation church).

By the time he left Dockery's, Patton was glib on the guitar, which he had picked up despite the harsh and sometimes brutal objections of his father, who considered the kind of "loose" music Charley favored blasphemous. But Patton's fascination with performing and his fondness for the attention it brought him, especially from women, was ample

His Caucasian features and scant resemblance to his father caused unkind talk about Charley Patton's heritage.

incentive to sidestep his father's determined efforts to derail his budding pursuit. Patton was encouraged by a local family named Chatmon, with whom he played for several years at various functions and gatherings in nearby towns. He also spent considerable time watching and mimicking a plantation picker named Henry Sloan, whose musical approach was far less demure than that of the Chatmons. Not much is known about Sloan except that he played country blues before the turn of the century and was therefore one of its earliest known proponents. Some believe Charley Patton learned how to "pick" in a blues style from Sloan, a departure from the strumming and thumping Patton did with the Chatmons.

Not remembered as an especially religious man, despite (or maybe because of) his father's efforts to the contrary, Patton was nevertheless torn between the pious, responsible life his parents urged on him and the life of a rambling musician. He actually gave up performing several times during his youth and took up studies for the ministry, but he always lapsed, unable to permanently stifle his nature as a rambler, drinker, and carouser. Besides blues, Patton recorded a large collection of religious songs. There is really no irony in that; these spirituals and hymns were among the first songs he learned on the plantation, and they stayed with him throughout his life. He performed the material in the same gruff and sometimes mongrel way as he performed the blues, often using a bottleneck or knife blade as a guitar slide. Songs such as "Prayer of Death," "It Won't Be Long," and "Oh Death," a duet with Bertha Lee (with whom he lived during the last four years of his life), demonstrate that Patton was a charismatic, even electrifying, religious singer. But his religious material was derivative; Patton's legacy is primarily that of a bluesman, not a gospel singer.

Following his separation from Dockery's, Patton led the life for which he had rehearsed throughout his adolescence: he worked wherever he could as an itinerant "hand," mostly in the timber trade, and entertained with his music on an equally itinerant basis. He entertained audiences that were both black and white,

Booker T. Washington "Bukka" White (1909–1977)

In his day, Bukka White was a sharecropper, convict, secondhand furniture dealer, and master of the Delta blues, but his first attempt at a career in music was a complete commercial failure. The "discovery" of his music in the 1960s by folk artists such as Bob Dylan, Buffy Sainte-Marie, John Fahey, and Bill Barth led to a second career for the Aberdeen, Mississippi, native that ultimately brought him the recognition that had eluded him as a younger man.

Although White was locally revered as an enormously talented bluesman, his fame never spread much beyond the Delta before the 1960s, despite several prewar recordings, including sessions with Alan Lomax for the Library of Congress. It wasn't until 1962 that White reemerged and became an international figure. In that year both Bob Dylan and Buffy Sainte-Marie recorded White's "Fixin' to Die," inspiring John Fahey and Bill Barth to launch a search for the obscure composer.

They found him in Aberdeen and were delighted to discover that he had remained a hearty and proficient player over the many years that had elapsed since he wrote "Fixin' to Die" and other masterpieces, such as "Parchman Farm" (named for the Mississippi state prison in which White was incarcerated more than once), "Panama Limited," and "Aberdeen Mississippi Blues." White, it turned out, was also willing to resume his previously unremunerative musical career, and he began touring and recording extensively throughout the remainder of the decade.

Bukka White's career choices were dictated by economic necessity. His early recordings, inexplicably, did not sell well and his opportunities to record shrank accordingly. He had some success as a sharecropper and evidently turned to used furniture sales as a means of making more money. Though he made his living at other pursuits, White continued to play and sing the blues for his own enjoyment throughout his life. More fortunate than many of his blues-playing contemporaries, White enjoyed wide acclaim for his music before his life ended.

in venues as diverse as plantation shacks, dance halls, "jook" joints, picnics, and the porches of "crossroads" stores. As he had done with the Chatmons, Patton occasionally entertained the white Mississippi gentry in the gardens and yards of their sprawling plantation homes.

Patton probably played a variety of music when he put on a show. His commercial recordings include gospel and spirituals, ballads, and folk tunes, and it's likely that all of those were also in his performance repertoire. Recollections are that Patton's recorded work is far more polished than his live performances, which were quite frenetic at times. (If so, he was unusual; the recorded performances of many early blues players often do not compare well in the assessment of those who heard the material played live.) Of course, Patton was not unusual in the theatrical antics he incorporated into his shows; the influence of these stunts, like that of the music itself, can be seen and

heard in the performances of today's blues and rock bands. He amused audiences by holding his guitar behind his back, on his head, or upside down on his shoulders, for instance, plunking out contorted solo parts while dancing around.

Blues is a supremely personal music that couldn't exist without the fuel of universal themes such as love, lust, passion, betrayal, injustice, and so on. Early blues players often localized as well as personalized their music, and Charley Patton was no exception. Many of his

Sam Chatmon encouraged the aspiring Charley Patton by bringing the young guitarist along to gigs in the Sunflower County vicinity.

blues centered on events he either witnessed or heard about as he grew up in the Delta; in fact, they are among the most "regional" blues ever written. Usually his characters were people he knew—friends, enemies, police, bootleggers, foremen, growers, and the like. The settings for many of his songs were immediately recognizable to his neighbors, and included mentions of rural towns, jails, attractions, and occurrences. (The blues are often invaluable texts that can evoke the past, often with astonishing accuracy. In fact, one Delta bluesman, Mississippi John Hurt, was located during the 1960s by a fan who used an early recording of Hurt's as a road map.)

Patton wrote about the devastating Delta flood of 1927 in "High Water Everywhere, Part 1 and 2." He told of his own prison experiences in "Tom Rushen Blues" and "High Sheriff Blues." But like the work of most Delta bluesmen, the bulk of his music was made up of brief, slice-of-life vignettes about the many mundane things poor folks experienced as they lived out their often grim lives. These events were aptly and succinctly observed in such songs as "Moon Goin' Down," "Revenue Man Blues," "Jersey Bull Blues," "Heart Like Railroad Steel," "Rattlesnake Blues," and "Love Is My Stuff."

For example, the small town of Belzoni, in Humphries County, Mississippi, figures prominently in Patton's "High Sheriff Blues." The song is Patton's lament about the hopelessness of being put on trial in Belzoni and the inevitability of a conviction there (a common enough sentiment among blacks in the Delta, who were routinely arrested, beaten, and tossed in prison often for no other reason than being on the street after a certain hour).

> *When the trial's in Belzoni, ain't no use*
> *screamin' and cryin',*
> *When the trial's in Belzoni, ain't no use to*
> *scream and cry,*
> *Mr. Ware will take you back to Belzoni*
> *jail house for life.*

Ware, the sheriff of Humphries County at the time, evidently spared every expense in the upkeep of his jail, at least to hear Patton describe it in the second verse.

Let me tell you folkses, how he treated me,
Let me tell you folkses, how he treated me,
And he put me in a cellar just as dark as
it could be.

A local man named Purvis, probably a planter, also appears in the song, possibly as a sympathetic figure who pleads with a man named Webb to "let poor Charley down," possibly a deputy of Sheriff Ware. It may also be that Purvis was the man who prosecuted Patton. It's a matter of interpreting the meaning of the final line of the third verse.

> *It was late one evening, Mr. Purvis was*
> *standin' 'round,*
> *It was late one evening, Mr. Purvis was*
> *standin' 'round,*
> *Mr. Purvis told Mr. Webb, sir, to let poor*
> *Charley down.*

Regardless of his actual role, Purvis is ultimately portrayed in the song's final verse as a distant, uncaring figure whose privileged life has little to do with that of the unfortunate singer.

> *When I was in trouble, you know no use*
> *to scream and cry,*

When I was in prison, ain't no use to
scream and cry,
Mr. Purvis in his mansion, he just don't
pay no mind.

Paramount Records in Chicago was the first to record Charley Patton commercially. Calling its line of disks aimed specifically at black consumers "The Popular Race Record," Paramount had carved out a lucrative market, mostly among southern blacks, and its representatives scoured the countryside for performers of blues, spirituals, and any other "nigger music" that might sell. (Following the success in 1920 of Mamie Smith's "Crazy Blues," a number of record companies started up "race record" divisions. Between 1920 and 1925 those divisions "discovered" and recorded some authentic country blues players such as Sylvester Weaver, a guitarist from the southeast who played a blues and ragtime mix, and Blind Lemon Jefferson, a Texan who became one of Paramount's earliest "race" artists.)

A music-store owner in Jackson, Mississippi, named Henry C. Spier was a Paramount agent who kept an eye on local

Mississippi John Hurt (1894–1966)

Another Delta musician "resurrected" during the folk movement of the 1960s, Mississippi John Hurt was, above everything else, a superb guitar player. Like Bukka White, Hurt made several recordings early in his life that went nowhere commercially, though unlike White, Hurt never pursued fame.

By chance he was recorded in the late 1920s by traveling scouts from Vocalion Records. As a result, he was later invited to record in New York under the direction of guitarist Lonnie Johnson. The tracks he recorded at this time were admired and circulated in a small circle of blues aficionados, but achieved no commercial success. The appeal of recording his music quickly faded for Hurt, who much preferred to remain on a Mississippi farm in the company of his large family.

Years later, folklorist Tom Hoskins went looking for Hurt, using the lyrics of the 1928 recording "Avalon, My Home Town" as a map. Flattered to have been sought out on the basis of records that were thirty-five years old, Hurt enjoyed several years on the concert trail late in life, impressing thousands with his reserved humor, sophisticated wit, and extraordinary playing and singing.

Not just a bluesman, Hurt is remembered as an all-purpose entertainer. He performed for his neighbors in Avalon and later for mostly young white blues and folk aficionados on college campuses and at the Newport Folk Festival. His extensive repertoire was arranged in a unique style that featured his thrilling fingerpicking. Later players such as John Fahey and Doc Watson credit Hurt as being a prime inspiration in their own musical development.

talent and passed along promising leads to the home office. Spier enthusiastically recommended Charley Patton to Arthur Laibley, one of Paramount's recording directors, who set up a session in Richmond, Indiana, at the Gennett Record Studio. Patton traveled there for the session, which was held June 14, 1929. He cut fourteen sides that Friday, in a variety of styles, and immediately headed back to Mississippi.

A month and a half later, Paramount released "Pony Blues" (b/w "Banty Rooster Blues"), promoting Charley Patton in black newspapers, such as the national black weekly out of Chicago, *The Defender*, as "the one and only Charley Patton." Almost immediately, Patton's religious number "Prayer of Death" (b/w "I'm Going Home") was also released, but on that record Paramount identified him as Elder J.J. Hadley, probably to avoid problems with buyers, many of whom would not purchase religious music that was performed by a blues singer. Lines had been starkly drawn in the debate about the sacred and the profane; just as they had been to Patton's father, blues and jazz seemed unquestionably sacrilegious to many devout or superstitious blacks. In a time of high evangelism, even folks who were not particularly religious felt uncomfortable listening to spirituals and gospel that were "tainted" by blues singers, who were often reviled as agents of the Devil.

Nor was that the last time Paramount purposely misidentified Patton. It is anyone's guess why he was billed as "The Masked Marvel" when the cut "Screamin' and Hollerin' the Blues" (b/w "Mississippi Bo Weevil Blues") was released in September of 1929. No mention was made of Charley Patton in the advertisements for the record, which depicted on its sleeve a dapper man in a tuxedo, wearing a mask.

Those records did well enough for Paramount to invite Patton to record sev-

Henry C. Spier heard and recommended many Delta players, including Charley Patton, Tommy Johnson, and Robert Johnson, to northern record labels.

eral more sides at the end of the year. He did the dates in Grafton, Wisconsin, with his friend Henry "Son" Sims, a black singer and fiddle player, and possibly with Willie Brown, who may have served as "commentator," a background vocal role that consisted of extemporaneously repeating verse snippets and adding brief, spoken observations. (Brown was eight or ten years younger than his mentor, Patton, and learned guitar from him. Brown quickly developed into a far more skilled player than his teacher, and later cut several solo records that convincingly demonstrate his impressive technique. Stylistically, however, Brown was never far away from Patton, and while his contributions to Patton's recordings are considerable, he is not remembered today as a true innovator.)

Not long after the trip to Grafton, while wandering in the upper Delta, Patton met the woman with whom he would live for the remaining four years of his life. Bertha Lee was a cook for a white family in Lula, Mississippi. (She was also a singer herself, and would later perform with Patton on the religious song "Oh Death" and record some of her own blues during Patton's final recording session in New York City.) At about the same time, in late 1929 or early 1930, the remarkable blues singer Eddie "Son" House wandered into Lula and befriended the couple. House and Patton began performing together, and Charley took him along to another recording session for Paramount, again in Wisconsin. Also part of the entourage were Willie Brown and Louise Johnson, a barrelhouse pianist and singer with whom Patton had a fling, though on the Grafton trip she paired off with House. It was at this session that Patton and Brown recorded two exemplary duets, "Moon Goin' Down" and "Bird Nest Bound."

Charley Patton died four years after the second Wisconsin session. In the intervening years he enjoyed celebrity status in the Delta, but in the days before royalties, he still had to work to make ends meet. He and Bertha Lee moved from Lula to Cleveland, near Dockery's, and finally to Holly Ridge, Mississippi. But his health was failing and he was almost killed by a knife-wielding man while giving a show in Merigold, Mississippi, an incident that left his throat scarred. (Random violence such as this was a familiar ingredient in Delta life. Musicians quickly learned to be especially careful about how they behaved. They were watchful for signs of resentment among audience members who begrudged their comparatively "easy" lifestyle, and most were especially wary of the roving eyes of women whose jealous spouses might also be nearby.)

Patton made no further recordings for Paramount after 1930, but, suffering and in ill health, he did cut some listless sides for the American Recording Company. As the Depression wound down, a representative of that label, recollecting Patton's popularity in 1930, sought him out and escorted him and Bertha Lee to New York City in January 1934.

Patton died April 28, 1934, in Indianola, Mississippi, not far from Dockery's. The official cause was given as mitral valve failure, possibly the result of a childhood case of rheumatic fever. Patton's life, for all his local celebrity,

hadn't been easy. His years of manual labor and heavy drinking, in addition to the countless other ways he abused himself, all took their toll. Not surprisingly for the time and place, his death was covered in neither the local nor national press. There is even the possibility that he had walked out on Bertha Lee in Holly Ridge in the final days of his life and died alone in Indianola. Whatever the circumstances, Charley Patton's life was paradigmatic for a Delta dweller and bluesman. His performances enlivened the harsh lives of those who heard him play. He inspired countless wide-eyed boys and girls and quite a few experienced guitar pickers, some of whom went on to make their own marks. It is through his music and his incredible legacy that Charley Patton's name will be forever linked with the birth of the Delta blues.

Son House

For two years before hooking up with Charley Patton in about 1930, Eddie James "Son" House, Jr. (1902–1988) had been a prisoner in the Mississippi state farm at Parchman, serving an indefinite term for murder. He had shot a man in 1928 during a drunken house party near his hometown of Lyon. House was fortunate enough to have won a pardon from an obliging judge, who strongly suggested that he leave the area, advice Son wasted no time heeding. It was during his retreat from the courthouse in Clarksdale that Son House wandered north into Lula, Mississippi (perhaps to visit relatives), where he met and befriended Charley Patton and Patton's common-law wife, Bertha Lee.

Twenty-eight or so years old at the time, House was just beginning to play slide guitar. He never became especially fluent on the instrument; his main strengths as a bluesman would be his vocals and his songwriting. Son's singing was distinctively embellished compared to the unadorned growls and shouts of other Delta blues players, and many of his songs, such as "Preachin' the Blues" and "My Black Mama," have vivid, haunting, and emotionally literate qualities—ingredients that made a spe-

Son House was torn between the Gospel and the blues. That conflict probably informed his powerful lyrics and impassioned singing style.

cial impression on a young player named Robert Johnson.

House suffered internal conflicts about music most of his life. Born on March 21 on a Coahoma County farm near Lyon, Mississippi, he was brought up religiously, and by his own admission, felt strongly as a young man that guitar players were practically messengers of Satan.

House was a regular churchgoer, sang in choirs, and preached in a Baptist church not far from his home. It's likely that if he had been told at the age of twenty that his legacy would be that of a premier exponent of Delta blues, he would never have believed it. But that's exactly what happened. By the time he was thirty years old, Son House had succumbed to whatever temptation the life of a bluesman held out, and he threw in his lot with Charley Patton, Willie Brown, and countless other players, contributing brilliantly to the development of a music he once feverishly despised. This combination may seem at first strange, but many bluesmen emerged from the religious sphere; Texan Blind Willie Johnson is one such example (although Johnson, unlike House, remained devout throughout his life).

House may have inherited his ambivalence regarding music from his father, who was an extremely religious man with an overpowering itch to make music, not necessarily in praise of the Lord. A horn player, House's father one day began entertaining locally in a band comprised mostly of his brothers. It would have been quite a shock to the young House if he ever saw his father's act, but it's not certain that he did. His parents separated when Son was a youngster; as it turned out, he went south with his mother to Tallulah, Louisiana, just across the river from Vicksburg, Mississippi.

As a teenager, House began a hard life of manual labor, picking moss from trees near Algiers, Louisiana, that was used like cotton in the manufacture of mattresses. After his mother died he began rambling through the Delta, up to Memphis, over to Arkansas, and down through Louisiana. He worked sporadically on a number of plantations, plowing, picking, and chopping cotton. He once took a job on a Louisiana cattle ranch, where he developed a fondness for wearing cowboy hats.

The great migration of rural southern blacks to the cities was well underway in the 1920s. Hard-pressed to survive in the often hostile Jim Crow South, tens of thousands of blacks were heading north,

Blind Willie Johnson (1890–1947)

Not really a bluesman in the strictest sense, Texas-born Blind Willie Johnson was a religious singer whose powerful voice and adroit slide guitar work were at least the equal of most bluesmen of his day. His style and intensity matched those of his Delta contemporaries, but his repertoire was strictly sacred.

His eyesight destroyed at age seven during an inexplicable attack by his stepmother, who threw sulfuric acid in his face, Johnson was limited in his choice of livelihoods. He became a Baptist preacher, spending most of his adult life as a street performer in and around the Texas communities of Waco and Dallas, preaching the gospel and singing spirituals.

During a search for religious singers, Columbia Records arranged a session with Johnson in 1927 at which he recorded many of the tunes for which he is remembered today. These included "Motherless Children," a superb showcase of his slide guitar prowess, and "Jesus Make Up My Dying Bed." Over the next three years Johnson recorded about thirty tracks for Columbia. He stopped recording altogether in 1930, preferring instead to concentrate on his "street ministry" in Waco.

Johnson perfected a unique guitar style in which he accompanied his singing with scattered but frequent solo riffs that were modulated by a slide, in a rapid high-note, low-note progression. His style influenced many guitarists over the years, especially the folk artists of the 1960s.

Blind Willie Johnson died tragically in 1947. Following a fire that completely destroyed his home in Waco, a local hospital, assuming he was uninsured, refused to treat him. Johnson had little choice but to return to his burned-out house, where he soon contracted pneumonia and died.

looking for opportunity. Some who had made the pilgrimage would later return for visits, bringing with them stories of tremendous prosperity. Their reports, sometimes exaggerated, inspired others who had been less adventuresome to pack up and go. So it was with Son House who, encouraged by friends, moved to St. Louis, Missouri, in the early twenties. He took a job at the Commonwealth Steel works in East St. Louis, Illinois, across the same river that nourished his native Delta several hundred miles to the south. His wage was a whopping one dollar an hour, princely compared to the scant money he had been earning as a manual laborer in Mississippi.

But House was a determined wanderer throughout his young life and he returned to the Delta after only a year or two in St. Louis. There he resumed his routine as an itinerant laborer until, in the late twenties, he stepped into a crowd in Matson, Mississippi, that had gathered to hear an impromptu performance by guitarists Willie Wilson and Ruben Lacy. Not much is known about Wilson, but Lacy was a budding local musical figure who had released several sides for Paramount in the late twenties, including "Mississippi Jailhouse Groan." That record in particular shows him to have been a competent slide guitar player and a brooding singer in the classic Delta blues style. Lacy was

also a gospel shouter, and perhaps it was that combination of musical magnetism and religious fervor that at once hooked House on the idea of becoming a bluesman himself.

The facts of House's apprenticeship are not clear, and recollections are contradictory. In a 1965 interview in New York City with music writer Julius Lester, House himself recalled that it was Willie Wilson whose slide guitar playing he admired that day, and that Wilson later taught him the rudiments of the style. Other researchers identify Ruben Lacy and an obscure picker named James McCoy as House's first teachers. It may have been that it was Wilson's guitar style that Son admired, and Lacy's vocal work; but whatever the inspiration, from that day forward, Son House buried as deeply as he could his lifelong aversion to "the Devil's music," and began his career as a Delta bluesman.

That career was almost immediately interrupted by the 1928 shooting incident, to which House pleaded self-defense. Two years later, after his release from Parchman farm, Son House met

Charley Patton and Bertha Lee in Lula, Mississippi, and traveled with Patton to Grafton, Wisconsin, for a Paramount recording session. There he backed Patton, who was a Paramount "star" by that time on the strength of "Pony Blues" and several other previous releases. Just as importantly, House recorded his own "Preachin' the Blues," "My Black Mama," and "Dry Spell Blues" in Grafton, three numbers that will always be thought of as classics of Delta blues. On that same date, he also recorded "Mississippi Country Farm" and "Clarksdale Moan," a duet with either Patton or Brown. He was paid forty dollars for the session, a sum that House later observed would have taken him at least a year to earn in the cotton fields.

"Preachin' the Blues" was probably an attempt by House to justify his abandonment of preaching to sing the blues, and it begins with a cynical attack on the clergy.

*Oh I'm gon' get me a religion, I'm gon'
    join the Baptist church,
Oh I'm gon' get me a religion, I'm gon'
    join the Baptist church,*

*I'm gon' be a Baptist preacher and I sure
    won't have to work.*

Despite this firm opening salvo, House waffles throughout the remainder of the song, clearly uncomfortable about the road he chose, blaming the decision on "women and whiskey." Ultimately he resolves that the blues is a "calling," very much like gospel.

*Oh, and I had religion, Lord, on this very
    day,
Oh, I had religion, Lord, this very day,
But the womens and the whiskey, well
    they would not let me pray....
Oh, I got to stay on the job, I got no time
    to lose,
Uhm, I ain't got no time to lose, I swear to
    God I got to preach these gospel blues.
(Spoken: Great God Almighty!)*

House remained in the Delta through the 1930s, playing wherever he could. He was revered and imitated by countless would-be bluesmen, including a youngster from Hazlehurst, Mississippi, named Robert Johnson. (Johnson was just a boy when he first encountered Son House but

The blues and folk revival of the 1960s briefly brought Son House out of a fifteen-year retirement that commenced with the death in 1948 of his only surviving Delta friend, fiddler Willie Brown.

was destined to display talents that would later astound all the early Delta players.) House left Mississippi in the early forties to take a job at a war supply factory in Rochester, New York. He then worked building railroad cars in East

Rochester, and later became a porter on the New York Central out of Buffalo.

Son House rarely played in public after leaving the Delta, and considered himself officially retired when his friend Willie Brown died, sometime in 1948. He was briefly lured back into the spotlight during the folk revival of the sixties, appearing mostly at colleges and festivals, but in his own mind he had long since retired his guitar. Eddie House, Jr., died in Detroit, Michigan, October 19, 1988.

Robert Johnson

The link between the simple, rural, acoustic blues of the Mississippi Delta and the ornate, guitar-based electrified blues that could be heard starting around 1940 in cities such as Memphis and Chicago was the slight, pensive, restless Mississippi guitar wizard named Robert Leroy Johnson (1911–1938). By augmenting the themes and styles of Delta mentors such as Son House, Charley Patton, and Willie Brown, Johnson created, by comparison, an intricate and sophisticated music that impressed both his teachers and his contemporaries. Some of his Delta peers, like Muddy Waters and Elmore James (1910–1963), took Johnson's lead to town, paving the way for a style called rhythm and blues, and later, an international musical phenomenon called rock and roll.

Robert Johnson spent most of his brief life pursuing and perfecting his craft as a bluesman and entertainer. Maybe to compensate for a childhood that was unusually complicated, he spent nearly all his life on the move, traveling mostly in the Mississippi Delta, but ranging as far afield as Canada and New York City. Everyone who knew him or ever saw him play would mention that his visits were brief, and his departures were hasty and mostly without cere-

mony. The connection has been made countless times between Johnson's furtive life and one of his blues masterpieces, "Hellhound on My Trail." There was also

It wasn't voodoo or a pact with the Devil that fueled Robert Johnson's brief but apocalyptic career. His fame and legacy were built on skill, inventiveness, keen observance of the reigning Delta guitar masters, and diligent practice.

a widespread rumor that Robert made a deal with the Devil, giving up his soul in exchange for his spectacular talent and eight years among the living to display it. Johnson did little to discourage that kind of talk and may even have promoted the stories to enhance his cachet, not unusual among some Delta musicians who seemed to enjoy the effect, especially on women, of their dangerous reputations. In "Me and the Devil Blues," Johnson sings, "Early this mornin', when you knocked upon my door. Early this mornin', when you knocked upon my door. And I said, 'Hello, Satan, I believe it's time to go.'"

This sort of invocation was absolutely believable to many of the illiterate and superstitious rural folk in the Delta. Other locally famous bluesmen, such as Tommy Johnson (possibly related distantly to

Fond of erotic themes and demonic characters, Peetie Wheatstraw (seen here with a custom-made guitar) was best known as a blues pianist and singer whose other- wise languid style reflected his St. Louis roots.

Robert) and William Bunch (1905–1941), who billed himself as Peetie Wheatstraw, told similar tales about themselves; Tommy Johnson always carried a large rabbit's foot charm, and Bunch referred to himself as "the Devil's Son-in-Law" or the "High Sheriff from Hell." Despite widespread conversion to Christianity, African and Caribbean religious myths still held sway in the minds of many blacks just as many other Americans indulged superstitions about black cats, the number thirteen, breaking mirrors, and walking under ladders. It was more or less a given in the Delta that on some nights, around midnight, at a lonely crossroads, a person could strike a deal with the Devil and thereby achieve fame (or some other desire) in exchange for his or her soul.

Johnson's "Cross Road Blues" is now a standard that has been recorded and reworked by a host of performers over the years including the great contemporary British blues guitarist Eric Clapton, whose early group Cream issued a powerful version called "Crossroads." The song does not describe any dealings with Satan, but it does paint a foreboding picture of impending doom in which God is petitioned for help, but is perhaps unable or unwilling to intervene.

> *I went to the crossroads, fell down on my*
> *knees*
> *I went to the crossroads, fell down on my*
> *knees*
> *Asked the Lord above "Have mercy, save*
> *poor Bob, if you please."*

> *You can run, you can run, tell my friend-*
> *boy Willie Brown*
> *You can run, tell my friend-boy Willie*
> *Brown*
> *Lord, that I'm standin' at the crossroad,*
> *babe I believe I'm sinkin' down.*

Robert Johnson was born in Hazlehurst, Mississippi, south of the Delta, on May 8, 1911. His mother was a short, sturdy woman named Julia, who was married to a successful furniture maker and black landowner named Charles Dodds, Jr. Dodds had not been in Mississippi when Robert had been conceived or born; he had been run out of the Hazlehurst area by a prominent white family named Marchetti, one of whom he had injured during an argument. Charles Dodds was in Memphis when Julia and a local man named Noah Johnson began an affair, the most tangible fruit of which was Robert, who would be dead before he turned thirty, but whose life and legacy would touch tens of millions of people.

Charles (left) and Julia Dodds (right) were married but not living in the same state when Julia conceived Robert Johnson during an affair with a Hazlehurst man.

In Tennessee, Dodds changed his name to C.D. Spencer and resumed making furniture. It's not clear why Julia did not accompany him to Memphis when he fled there around 1907; the two obviously remained in touch because Julia eventually joined him, about seven years later, bringing the toddler Robert along. She may have delayed going to Tennessee because she knew that Dodds' home was crowded. Once he had settled, Dodds had sent for his mistress, Serena, and their two sons. He had also sent for several of his six daughters by Julia. Whatever the reasons, Julia had remained in Mississippi, and after bearing Robert, had spent several hard years in migrant labor camps before trekking north to Memphis sometime around 1914. She didn't stay long, taking off again for Mississippi, leaving Robert with Charles and Serena.

Robert was given the surname Spencer and remained in Memphis until around 1918. At that time, his "father," not willing to contend with Robert's strong-willed behavior, sent him back to his mother, who by then had settled in Robinsonville, Mississippi, about forty miles away. Whether she and Charles ever divorced is unclear, but Julia had in the meantime married a field hand named Willie Willis. With Willis' help, she raised Robert to manhood.

Fascinated with music at an early age, Robert played Jew's harp as a youngster, trading licks with his chum R.L. Windum. He soon took up harmonica and could be found most days and nights hanging around the local guitar pickers, watching and listening intently, picking up the unique rhythms and inflections of Delta blues. By the late 1920s, Robert had taken up guitar.

The talented bluesman Willie Brown had moved near Robinsonville by 1916, and he generously tutored the teenager, sharing tips and techniques. (Robert himself was far less generous as a teacher. Even before he began his recording and performing career, he would sometimes abruptly leave a room, in the middle of a number, if he felt someone was scrutinizing his tech-

R.L. Windum was a childhood friend of Robert Johnson and an early musical collaborator with the blues giant.

nique too closely.) The great Charley Patton was also a regular visitor to Robinsonville, traveling up the short distance from Lula to visit and play with his good friend Brown and also to romance a local pianist, Louise Johnson. Patton and Brown, occasionally joined by Son House after his 1930 release from prison, were not at all surprised to see the young Robert among the late-night crowd of revelers at any house party or similar function at which they entertained. Son House in particular was a favorite of Robert's; Johnson admired the elder man's fierce performances and crisp, clear slide guitar work. Son was sometimes helpful as a teacher, showing Robert fingering and chording, and it's not surprising that several of Robert's own numbers, "Walkin' Blues" and "Preachin' Blues" for example, are based solidly on House's style.

At the age of seventeen, Robert married a

Lonnie Johnson (1894–1970)

Often overlooked in discussions about jazz, blues, and rock music, Lonnie Johnson was a pivotal figure in the development of each, particularly in the emergence of the guitar as a solo instrument in popular ensembles. Early Delta blues masters such as Skip James and Robert Johnson imitated his guitar work; great jazz players such as Louis Armstrong, Duke Ellington, and Eddie Lang clamored for his help in concerts and on records; modern bluesmen such as B.B. King and T-Bone Walker acknowledge their debt to Johnson's innovations; and "classic blues" singers such as Bessie Smith, Victoria Spivey, Clara Smith, and Texas Alexander all benefited from his accompaniment. Johnson's most significant contribution was the guitar solo. His remarkable dexterity on the instrument astounded all who heard him play. Using a pick, Johnson unleashed blistering solo riffs that were impossibly complex but astoundingly clear. He followed those with held "blue" notes and quick arpeggios. The combination was revolutionary at the time Johnson introduced it. Adopted by countless players over the years, the technique has become almost cliché, but its overwhelming acceptance opened the door for subsequent innovations, and Johnson is credited with establishing the guitar as a primary solo instrument.

Born in New Orleans, Lonnie Johnson traveled widely and almost constantly throughout his life. He recorded extensively, both as a solo artist and as a guitarist with the biggest names in blues and jazz. Dismissed as an anachronism during the blues and folk revivals of the 1960s, Johnson nevertheless left a monumental legacy as an innovator on the guitar and a purveyor of exceptionally sophisticated instrumental music.

fifteen-year-old girl named Virginia Travis, who soon after became pregnant. From all accounts he was pleased with the match and enthusiastically accepted the role of doting husband and expectant father. The couple moved in with Robert's half-sister, Bessie, who was living with her husband on the Klein plantation just outside of town. Tragically, both Virginia and the baby died in childbirth in April 1930. Not long afterward Robert left Robinsonville, telling friends he was headed south to Hazlehurst, his birthplace, hoping to find his biological father, Noah Johnson.

Robert spent about three years in the area around Hazlehurst, but it is not likely that he located his father. He fathered a child, Claud Johnson, now a successful businessman, and met and married an older woman named Caletta Craft. He spent most of his time playing guitar and listening to the records of established blues players such as Lonnie Johnson (no relation), Tommy Johnson (1896–1956), who lived in nearby Crystal Springs, and Scrapper Blackwell (1906–1962), whose single-string

Leroy Carr (sitting) and Scrapper Blackwell (standing) were two innovative musicians whose considerable contributions to the blues lived on through Robert Johnson.

picking style Robert assimilated. Johnson had for years admired the records of an old bluesman named Leroy Carr (1905–1935) who had a gift for melody and some unusual ideas about chord progressions. Even as a boy, Robert would play along on Jew's harp to Carr's hit record, "How Long Blues."

Except for Tommy Johnson, who lived in the area and who Johnson may have encountered personally, Robert's blues studies in Hazlehurst were almost entirely based on phonograph records. He also met and befriended an older bluesman named Ike Zinnerman from Grady, Alabama, who had migrated to Hazlehurst by 1930. Zinnerman never made records and his style and focus remain forever unknowable. It's likely that having grown up east of Mississippi, Zinnerman was inclined toward tuneful and melodic playing rather than the Delta's harsh, insistent drone. But there's no question about his reputation as a skillful player, and there's also little doubt that Robert Johnson wouldn't have given Zinnerman the time of day if he had thought there was nothing to be learned from him. As it was, Johnson visited the older man frequently, often spending long hours picking up pointers during all-night jams. Johnson, who

Callie Craft doted on Robert Johnson despite the fact that the guitarist abandoned her.

rarely sustained friendships, stayed in touch with Zinnerman for several years after the "roots" sojourn to Hazlehurst.

He began a routine of careful study followed by equally assiduous practice. Not exactly a prodigy (or an agent of Satan), Robert honed his guitar skills to their impressive and seemingly effortless edge through concerted practice. Associates tell of the long hours he would spend, working and reworking numbers he had heard, always in private, until he was satisfied that the music sounded exactly right.

When he returned to the Delta, Johnson was cocky and self-assured, and not at all reluctant to display the skills that his intensive study and practice had sharpened. His effortless way with complex guitar phrasings, the way he kept time by flailing his legs and stomping a syncopated percussion accompaniment, and his effortless vocals, which swooped dramatically into a piercing falsetto, astounded nearly everyone, including the masters House, Patton, and Brown. No one could figure how Robert had managed to improve so dramatically in such a short period of time. It was about then that the rumor of his pact with the Devil began making the rounds, and as if to underscore its potency, Robert commenced a rambling existence that kept him in no particular place longer than a few weeks at a stretch. He was like a specter, appearing at picnics, "jook" joints, house parties, and the like, up and down the Delta. He was there, he put on an astonishing show, and then he was gone.

Johnson abandoned Callie Craft and her three children by a previous marriage. Once he hit the road, his whereabouts were rarely communicated to Callie, who returned to Hazlehurst and died not long after. Averse to any kind of work except his music, Johnson learned early that women were an excellent and reliable source of support. His facility and relationships with women were well known in the Delta; his routine when arriving in a spot where he thought he might remain for longer than a few days was to charm his way into the bed of a local woman, who more often than not was also willing to provide board.

Like most performers, Johnson had more than his share of "groupies." But in the Delta, a performer could quickly lose his fingers, or even his life, at the hands of a jealous boyfriend or husband, or even a drunken plantation worker seething at the comparatively easy life of bluesmen. Friends warned Robert often enough to be careful about his flirtations, advice that typically went unheeded. It may have been a jealous husband who was behind Johnson's death in August of 1938, a death by poison that was slow and excruciating, stretching out over several days.

There are rumors upon rumors about the circumstances surrounding Robert Johnson's demise. Some say Satan's hellhound finally caught him; others claim he was knifed by a jealous woman. But the version generally thought to be the most accurate comes from a friend of Johnson's, musician Houston Stackhouse, as reported by Johnson historian Stephen

A disciple of Tommy Johnson, Houston Stackhouse was a perennial in the blues clubs of Memphis, Helena, and Chicago, and was a teacher to many second-generation blues players.

C. LaVere. The somewhat gruesome tale begins on Saturday night, August 13, 1938, at "Three Forks," a bump in the road east of Greenwood, Mississippi.

For a week or so beforehand Robert and another bluesman named Honeyboy Edwards (b. 1915) had been in the vicinity, playing a number of "jook" joints in and around Greenwood. As was his custom, Robert had befriended a woman; as it turned out, she was married to the man who ran the "Three Forks," where he and Honeyboy were to play on August 13. Also appearing that night was Sonny Boy Williamson II (1910–1965), and it's likely the evening was a rave. As Stackhouse tells it, though he himself was not present that night, Johnson began paying far too much attention to his new female friend, whose husband, the proprietor, began to get increasingly angry. Sonny Boy noticed, too, and having seen too many such situations turn ugly during his life, was on his guard. When a half-pint of whiskey with a broken seal was brought to the players, Sonny Boy slapped it away, admonishing the younger man never to drink from an opened bottle. But Johnson, reckless literally to the end, disregarded Sonny Boy's advice and drank heartily from another opened bottle of liquor that arrived soon thereafter.

It wasn't long before Johnson began to display all the symptoms of a poison victim. Taken to a nearby room retching and immobile, he later became delirious. His youth and strength were apparently enough to fend off the effects of the poison (probably strychnine). Shortly afterward, however, Johnson contracted something that may have been pneumonia. He died (without seeing a doctor) the following Tuesday, August 16.

In the five years between his triumphant return to the Delta from Hazlehurst as a skilled, confident musician and his grizzly death near Greenwood, Johnson led life at a furious pace, appearing nearly everywhere in the Delta. He also performed in the wide-open town of Helena, Arkansas, the closest thing he had to a home base, which by the mid-1930s was the capitol of the Delta blues. He made his first recordings in November 1936 for the American Record Company (ARC), the same outfit that had put Charley Patton's final sessions on disk two years earlier. The go-between was H.C. Spier of Jackson, the man who had recommended Patton to his first label, Paramount, in the late 1920s. Johnson approached Spier directly, and was recommended by him to Ernie Oertle of ARC. After auditioning Johnson, Oertle took him to San Antonio to record under the supervision of an ARC executive named Don Law. On Monday, November 23, 1936, Johnson made his first recordings, including "Terraplane Blues," "I Believe I'll Dust My Broom," "Sweet Home Chicago," and "Kind Hearted Woman Blues." In four subsequent recording sessions that year and the next, Johnson committed to wax his entire discography. Happily, all of it survives to this day, including "Cross Road Blues," "If I Had

Sonny Boy Williamson II, a.k.a. Rice Miller, never told the same story twice about when and where he was born.

Possession Over Judgment Day," "From Four Until Late," and "Love in Vain Blues," a hit for the Rolling Stones more than thirty years after it was first recorded.

Surprisingly, of all the records Johnson made for ARC, only "Terraplane Blues" (about a flashy automobile) was a respectable seller, and the company stopped calling him to record after his fifth session, on June 20, 1937, in Dallas. Johnson spent most of the last year of his life traveling, embarking on a lengthy roadtrip with Johnny Shines (1915–1992) and Calvin Frazier to St. Louis, Decatur, Chicago, Detroit, Windsor (Canada), New York, New Jersey, and back to Mississippi through Memphis.

On the road he met, or renewed acquaintanceships with, musicians such as pianists Roosevelt Sykes and Peetie Wheatstraw (who also played guitar), and discovered that quite a few people had heard of him, even very far from his home.

Blues buffs will always speculate about what direction Johnson would have taken had his life not ended at the age of twenty-seven. He was rumored to have begun performing with a small ensemble (piano and drums) just before his death. Even if he hadn't, it is likely that he would eventually have gotten around to an ensemble sound

A traveling companion of Robert Johnson, Johnny Shines was a gifted lyricist and performer whose career did not take off until late in his life despite his considerable talent and dedication to Delta blues.

had he lived, and explored every nuance of it, just as he had exhaustively explored and built upon the Delta blues. There is no doubt that his fame and influence would have increased dramatically; he was on John Hammond's list of performers for the landmark 1938 From Spirituals to Swing concert at Carnegie Hall. Hammond, the renowned talent scout, critic, and record producer, was aware of Johnson and sufficiently impressed to invite him to perform on a bill with the finest talent of the day. But Hammond's invitation came too late. By the time it arrived in Mississippi via Don Law, Robert Johnson was already in the ground beside the Little Zion Church, not far from Greenwood.

By the time of his death, Robert Johnson had effectively transcended the rural Delta blues he had grown up with, and was casting about for alternatives. His many experiences on the road with innovative musicians from other parts had opened up exciting new possibilities, and it is likely that his own keen creativity would have built upon them substantially. But fate passed the baton to others—some of them peers, some of them yet to be born. As it happened, the main innovator in the transformation of Delta blues into the searing, heart-pounding, electrified ensemble music called Chicago blues was practically a neighbor of Johnson's. Only four years younger and a rabid admirer of Robert, McKinley Morganfield was a Mississippi field hand, guitar player, bootlegger, and "jook" joint operator who went on to pioneer the music that ultimately gave birth to rhythm and blues, and not long afterward, rock and roll.

Muddy Waters

Born April 4, in Rolling Fork, on the Delta's southern tier, McKinley Morganfield (1915–1983) was raised by his maternal grandmother from about the age of six months, when his parents separated. It was his grandmother who nicknamed him "Muddy" because of his delight in splashing around in and eating the rich, black Delta soil. Later, his playmates on the Stovall plantation near Clarksdale, in Coahoma County, tacked on "Waters" when, at about the age of three, he and his grandmother moved up there from Rolling Fork.

Waters had a conventional childhood for the region; he helped his grandmother with chores, worked in the cotton fields, attended church, did some preaching, and amused himself and his friends by playing Jew's harp and harmonica. In a recollection given to writer Robert Palmer for the book *Deep Blues*, Waters claimed that he had cultivated an impressive sound on harmonica (which he called "French harp") by the age of nine. He describes playing as a boy with his friend Scott Bohannon, a guitarist, at fish fries, picnics, and other gatherings, to good effect. At about the age of seventeen, Waters ordered his first guitar, a Stella, from the Sears and Roebuck catalog, paying two dollars and fifty cents for it with part of his share of the proceeds from the sale of the family's last horse.

A prime force in the development and perfection of electrified Chicago blues, Muddy Waters moved to the Windy City in 1943, having spent almost all his young life on a Mississippi plantation.

Like any young man with an interest in music, Muddy would see the traveling musicians who appeared frequently on the plantation or at nearby venues. He listened to phonograph records of the leading musical figures of the day, local and regional players such as Blind Lemon Jefferson, Memphis Minnie, LeRoy Carr, and Lonnie Johnson. He also heard the music of sophisticated urban

Blind Lemon Jefferson (1897–1930)

One of the early purveyors of Texas blues, Blind Lemon Jefferson spent most of his life as a street singer and recording artist. Though he played and sang in a musical form that already existed, Jefferson nevertheless was an important contributor to the blues, which in his heyday was still taking shape in the South.

Scores of later blues players were influenced by Jefferson's flamenco-like guitar style, borrowed from the Mexican *vaqueros* who regularly wandered through Texas. Similarly, his high-pitched singing style was likely inspired by the chants of black cotton workers whose traditional field songs rang out daily in the agricultural areas of the state.

Blind since birth, Jefferson traveled many times to Chicago to record for Paramount. In the four years from 1926 to 1929, he recorded more than eighty songs, including "Match Box Blues," "See That My Grave Is Kept Clean," "Jack of Diamonds," and "Broke and Hungry." Many of his songs were later recorded by musical giants of the 1960s and 1970s such as Bob Dylan and Lightnin' Hopkins. The San Francisco rock band Jefferson Airplane came up with its name as a tribute to him.

Jefferson died tragically in Chicago during the winter of 1929. Disoriented during a snowstorm that blanketed the city, he froze to death as he tried to find his way home after an evening with friends.

jazz and blues performers. But it was the Delta guitar work of Robert Johnson he admired most. Waters was also deeply impressed by the vocal intensity and fierceness of Johnson's mentor, Son House.

Outside the Delta, by the mid-1930s, jazz had already been transformed a number of times since its beginnings in big southern cities, principally New Orleans, into a quirky amalgamation of pop, folk, and classical music. The first jazz bands to appear around the turn of the century were made up of an unlikely assortment of instruments, usually banjo, guitar, double-bass (or tuba), and perhaps a clarinet and a brass instrument or two. By the mid-1920s, jazz had shed its vaudeville trappings to become a soloist's medium, largely because of the skill of instrumentalists such as sax player Sidney Bechet (1897–1959) and trumpeter Louis Armstrong (1900–1971).

Ten years later, by the mid-1930s, the swing era was in full bloom and the quaint New Orleans style seemed passé, blown out by the slick, sophisticated, and powerful arrangements of the leading big bands. But like dinosaurs, the big bands died out quickly, never to return, killed by changing tastes and the deprivations and shortages of World War II. It was nearly impossible to keep large outfits together in a time of conscription, gas rationing, and heavy taxes on nonessentials, including a 20-percent "amusement tax." A strategically inept strike by the American Federation of Musicians (AFM) also figured prominently in the demise of the big bands;

A giant of both blues and jazz, Big Bill Broonzy had a career that was both long and prosperous.

ordered by their union not to make records because some jukebox owners and radio stations refused to pay royalties, AFM members quickly found themselves with no place to play during the difficult war years. Bebop was coming together under the auspices of innovators like Dizzy Gillespie (1917–1992) and Charlie Parker (1920–1955), whose "modern" jazz was developing into a music for appreciative audiences rather than merely a lubricant for parties.

Chicago's music scene thrived before and during World War II. The city was the end of the line for tens of thousands of migrating Southern blacks who enlivened the local scene as both players and consumers. Maxwell Street was alive with itinerants, playing for change; house parties and rent parties were held just as they had been "down home," but instead of a "jook" joint or plantation shotgun shack, the venues were Chicago tenements or somebody's back room. Brilliant instrumentalists such as Lionel Hampton (b. 1913) and Louis Jordan (1908–1978) were laying the groundwork for rhythm and blues with their boogie-based stomps, the most breathless of which, Hampton's 1942 hit "Flying Home" for example, featured blaring, primal saxophone riffs.

Commercially, blues music in Chicago was the purview of Columbia Records and Victor's Bluebird label. Both companies relied upon a white promoter named Lester Melrose to scout and produce talent, issuing records by players such as Mississippi's Robert Nighthawk (1919–1967), Tommy McClennan (1908–1962), Robert Petway, Arthur "Big Boy" Crudup (1905–1974), and Big Bill Broonzy (1898–1958). Other popular stars were Tampa Red (1903–1981) from Georgia; John Lee "Sonny Boy" Williamson (1914–1948) from Tennessee; Washboard Sam (1906–1966) from Arkansas; and the irrepressible Memphis Minnie. The "Bluebird Beat" was shorthand in those days for a driving sound, propelled mostly by a heavy bass line and thumping drums.

Known in his time as "The Guitar Wizard," Tampa Red was among the first blues players to adapt and widely popularize the clear glissando slide-guitar style of turn-of-the-century Hawaiian guitarists.

Memphis Minnie (1896–1973)

The undisputed queen of Chicago Blues between 1930 and 1950, Memphis Minnie (born Lizzie Douglas) was a powerful singer of tough, rural blues who, along with Big Bill Broonzy and Tampa Red, did much to define the Chicago style that paved the way for the subsequent generation of players that included Muddy Waters and Little Walter. Unlike earlier female singers of the more sedate "classic" blues such as Ida Cox and Bessie Smith, Memphis Minnie had a raucous drawl that was an ideal ingredient in the amplified grit of Chicago blues.

An accomplished guitarist, Memphis Minnie began her career at a young age in her native Memphis, singing and playing on streetcorners. She cut her first record in 1929, and in 1930 she had her first hit with the blues classic "Bumble Bee." Married by then to bluesman Kansas Joe McCoy, Minnie moved with her husband to Chicago in the early 1930s. They soon divorced, but not before achieving some success as a duo. McCoy pursued a solo career even as he was appearing with his wife, and after their separation, he and his brother, Charlie McCoy, went on to become the toast of Chicago clubs in a band called the Harlem Hamfats. Their appeal was such that even the gangster Al Capone became a fan.

It was during her association with Ernest "Little Son Joe" Lawlar that Memphis Minnie perfected her biting Chicago style. She married Lawlar in the mid-1930s, and the duo achieved tremendous success and popularity with hits such as "I'm So Glad," "Black Rat Swing," and "In My Girlish Days."

Minnie and Lawlar were friendly and supportive to the new generation of players coming up in Chicago. In the postwar years they were mentors to—and eventually eclipsed by—the powerful electrified blues bands led by Muddy Waters and others. Memphis Minnie retired from music when her husband died in 1957. She faded from sight and spent her final years in a nursing home, nearly forgotten.

Chicago was also the mecca for gospel music, centered by then at Thomas Andrew Dorsey's Pilgrim Baptist Church. Gospel was fast becoming a major cultural force, especially among blacks. A former blues pianist from Georgia, Dorsey (1899–1993) spent time in the 1920s as an arranger and accompanist for Bessie Smith and Gertrude "Ma" Rainey. He also cowrote with Tampa Red the sexually suggestive blues hits "Pat That Bread" and "Tight Like That." But by the 1930s Dorsey had been "saved," and he began a new career as lead evangelist on the "gospel highway," preaching in tents and churches throughout the country, often accompanied by gospel legends such as Roberta Martin (1907–1969) and Mahalia Jackson (1911–1972). With his assistant, Sallie Martin (1896–1988), Dorsey contributed hundreds of songs to the gospel canon, including "Precious Lord, Take My Hand," a song that became an anthem of the civil rights movement when it was requested by the Reverend Martin Luther King, Jr., shortly before his assassination at the hands of James Earl Ray.

Muddy Waters entered that cacophony in 1943, moving to Chicago from Mississippi after a brief taste of city life in St. Louis in 1940. Before heading north again, Waters ran a "jook" joint on Stovall's Plantation, complete with moonshine, gambling, a well-stocked jukebox, and an empty stage any time he wanted one. He was recorded twice on Stovall's by blues researcher Alan Lomax, in 1941 and 1942, each time for the Library of Congress. Those sessions, eventually released on the Testament label as *Down on Stovall's Plantation*, were tremendously encouraging to Waters, who despite a growing reputation had never before heard himself play and sing. He evidently liked what he heard, telling *Rolling Stone* magazine, "I sounded just like anybody's records. I carried that record up to the corner and put it on the jukebox. Just played it and played it and said, 'I can do it, I can do it!'"

In Chicago, Muddy busied himself at first with finding a job—not a difficult thing during wartime—and then by making the acquaintance of other Chicago musicians. He accomplished this by

Respected by audiences and peers alike, Sunnyland Slim helped redefine Chicago blues in association with players such as Muddy Waters and Little Walter.

doing the same things he'd done back home: he performed at house parties and other familiar but usually low-paying gigs. Muddy was luckier than a lot of new arrivals in the big city; his reputation as a competent blues man had preceded him to Chicago via friends, a few relatives, and others who had heard him in Mississippi and who had made the move to Chicago first. By day Muddy drove a truck, and at night he picked up whatever musical work he could find, usually through a network of friends or friends of friends. That was his routine for the first year or two. A highlight for him must have been the gift of an electric guitar in 1944 from an uncle. It was his first brush with an instrument that was essential for a musician to be heard over the din of big city nightlife, and, as it happened, the instrument with which he became a giant of Chicago blues.

It was in 1945 or 1946 that Waters landed what turned out to be his date with destiny at a South Side club called The Flame. It was the highest-paying music job he'd gotten since arriving in Chicago, about fifty dollars a week, to accompany his piano playing friend Eddie Boyd (b. 1914) and a lead guitarist named Blue Smitty on uptempo blues numbers and slick ballads à la Nat "King" Cole. During their run, Boyd took off for a higher- paying engagement, and the trio was joined by the veteran pianist, Sunnyland Slim, a.k.a. Albert Luandrew (1907–1995). A fellow Mississippian, Slim was several years older than Waters and extremely well-connected in town because of his talent and no-nonsense approach to music. It was

Leadbelly (1885–1949)

Larger-than-life character Leadbelly (a.k.a. Walter Boyd or Huddie Ledbetter) is remembered much more as a folk singer than as a bluesman. Author of the perennial favorite "Goodnight, Irene" and many other such songs, Leadbelly led an eventful life of mythic proportions that took him from the brothels of Shreveport to the garrets of Paris and Greenwich Village, New York.

A large, powerful man, Leadbelly was evidently also ornery. In 1917 he was sentenced to thirty years in prison for murdering a man with whom he had quarreled over a woman. It was in Angola Penitentiary that he was found by John and Alan Lomax of the Library of Congress during one of their many musicological expeditions in the South. Through their efforts, Leadbelly was released from prison to become their chauffeur; later, also with their encouragement, he became a familiar presence in the folk and blues clubs of New York City.

Leadbelly's repertoire was vast, comprising all kinds of music from lullabies and laments to country blues and cowboy songs. He began performing in Greenwich Village folk clubs, the purview of the likes of Pete Seeger and Woody Guthrie, in the mid-1930s. Music historians complain that whatever unique southern cant Leadbelly may have had in his early days was literally whitewashed during the period in which he performed in urban folk circles.

Whatever his musical legacy, there is no question that through his appearances in clubs and concerts on two continents, Leadbelly opened doors for blacks that had never even been ajar before.

through Sunnyland that Waters came to the attention first of the promoter Lester Melrose, and then of two Polish immigrants named Leonard and Phil Chess, whose Aristocrat record label would soon become world-famous among blues, rhythm and blues, and soul music fans as Chess Records, thanks in large part to Muddy Waters.

Through Melrose, in 1946, Sunnyland and Waters recorded a couple of tracks for Columbia Records that were never released. The following year, a talent scout for the Chess brothers named Sammy Goldstein decided to extend Aristocrat's repertoire into blues. The record company was a fledgling extension of the Chess brothers' otherwise bustling nightclub business; the pair had arrived in Chicago from Poland at the end of the 1920s, and by 1946 they had built up a string of nightclubs that featured live music, mostly jazz and slick, "classic" blues. Aristocrat's artist roster consisted mostly of jazz players, and Goldstein wanted to test the commercial appeal of blues. He asked Sunnyland to arrange the session.

Sunnyland, Waters, and bass player Big Crawford gathered soon afterward at the Universal Studio in downtown Chicago, cutting several songs: two tracks that featured Sunnyland ("Johnson Machine Gun" and "Fly Right, Little Girl") and two that featured Muddy. Waters wasn't expecting a featured spot but he was ready with two original blues, "Little Anna Mae" and "Gypsy Woman." In later years Muddy and Leonard Chess would form a close and trusting relationship, but at the outset of their association, Chess evidently didn't think much of the big Mississippian. He hesitated for several months before releasing Muddy's two tracks, and even then didn't promote them. The consensus among researchers and blues buffs is that Leonard Chess just didn't "get" blues. It was not that he had any reluctance about Muddy Waters—it was more that he was baffled by the music.

But Aristocrat called Muddy again, and this time he brought along his bottleneck slide and ran through a number of blues from the Delta, including several he had played for Alan Lomax back at

Stovall's. Leonard Chess was again mystified, but nevertheless released "I Can't Be Satisfied" (b/w "I Feel Like Going Home"), an issue that promptly sold out. Muddy Waters had his first hit record. It was based almost completely on his Delta traditions, and it swept through Chicago's black neighborhoods and into the South in a great big hurry. The next year, 1948, also through Sunnyland Slim, Waters took part in a recording session for Sunnyland's new label, Tempo Tone, that paired Muddy for the first time with the harmonica player "Little Walter" Jacobs (1931–1968). The results of the session were unspectacular, but the precedent was set for the kind of musical lineup Muddy would favor in the banner years ahead.

With his fame on the rise, Muddy organized a more or less full-time performance band comprised of himself on electric slide and vocals, Little Walter on harmonica, Jimmy Rogers (b. 1924) on guitar, and "Baby Face" LeRoy Foster playing both drums and guitar. (Elgin Evans was added on drums two years later.) The outfit rocked Chicago's clubs

A key figure in the development of Chicago blues, Little Walter was a singer, a songwriter, and a masterfully innovative harmonica player.

with its straight-ahead electrified Delta blues—raw, uncompromising, and rude as you please. After years of the slick, sultry, "jump" and "classic" blues, audiences sat up and took notice. It was a driving, macho sound with an evil edge that appealed to both sexes. But Leonard Chess, for reasons that were unfathomable and probably rooted in his deeply superstitious nature, refused to record Muddy's new band until 1951. Hits such as "Rollin' And Tumblin',"

Prolific as a songwriter and brilliant as both an arranger and record producer, Willie Dixon made incalculable contributions to the blues idiom.

recorded between 1948 and 1950, were done with an alternate lineup acceptable to Chess that included Big Crawford, who had played on Muddy's first hit.

Chess eventually relented, and in 1951, Muddy and his band had hits with "Honey Bee," "Louisiana Blues," "Long Distance Call," and "She Moves Me," defining Chicago blues. Instantly, the band became the outfit to be emulated by pure blues musicians coast to coast. Little Walter hit the national rhythm and blues charts for the first time for his featured harmonica part in "Louisiana Blues," which was also the second release for the new Chess Records label (the first was

Muddy's "Rollin' Stone," an adaptation of "Catfish Blues," a song that for a time was his signature work).

Among Muddy's new fans was a bass player named Willie Dixon (1915–1992), who had done some work at Aristocrat for Leonard Chess. Dixon was also a gifted songwriter and he wasted no time approaching Muddy with a few of his tunes. Recognizing brilliance when he heard it, Muddy accepted the material and in 1954 had the biggest successes of his career with Dixon's "I'm Your Hoochie Coochie Man," "I'm Ready," and "Just Make Love to Me" (often called "I Just Wanna Make Love to You").

Muddy Waters died in his sleep in 1983. In the twenty-nine years between 1954, when he had his first national hits, and 1983, his career took a number of ups and downs. Almost immediately after their national successes, members of his band (called the Headhunters) drifted away to pursue their own dreams of stardom. An incidental tune called "Juke," recorded in 1952 by Muddy, Elgin Evans, Jimmy Rogers, and featuring Little Walter on harmonica, became the number one rhythm and blues song in the country, hovering at the top spot for four months. It far surpassed any recording success that Muddy himself had yet attained, and prompted Little Walter to form his own band, though he continued to record occasionally with the Headhunters.

Over the years musicians came and went. Among Waters' alumni are players as eminent as Elmore James, Otis Spann, Junior Wells, Buddy Guy, Walter Horton,

The record labels owned by Leonard Chess (above) and his brother Phil were instrumental in the international spread of blues, jazz, and gospel.

James Cotton, Luther Johnson, and Earl Hooker. A 1958 appearance in England electrified audiences, and developments there in the aftermath no doubt greatly affected more than a few of the budding musicians who would soon lead the "British Invasion" of the United States during the 1960s. When it came, the invasion featured a lot of the music written by Muddy, his peers, and his forebears.

During a lull in his career, Waters returned to England in 1972 and recorded an album with four leading lights: Rory Gallagher, Steve Winwood, Rich Grech, and Jimi Hendrix's drummer Mitch Mitchell. The result, *The London Muddy Waters Sessions*, was more a novelty than a breakthrough. Waters was finding it difficult to locate musicians who could handle his apparently straightforward but actually highly nuanced style of blues. It was the white Texas guitarist Johnny Winter who pulled Waters out of semiretirement in 1976, tirelessly organizing what would become a series of four albums for Blue Sky Records that properly and masterfully showcased Muddy's mature style.

The Grammy-winning *Hard Again* was released in 1976, featuring Waters, Winter, and former Headhunter James Cotton. Two other former Headhunters, Jimmy Rogers and Walter Horton, were recruited for 1978's *I'm Ready*, followed the next year by *Muddy "Mississippi" Waters Live*. His final album for Blue Sky, *King Bee*, was released in 1978. It was around that time that Muddy made a show-stopping appearance at a farewell concert for Bob Dylan's former outfit, The Band, at San Francisco's Fillmore West. Muddy blew through an impassioned "Mannish Boy" in the "stop-time" tempo that he had created with Willie Dixon, inspiring obvious awe among the music industry superstars who accompanied him. The concert was filmed by director Martin Scorsese and released as *The Last Waltz*.

Despite those considerable achievements late in his career, Waters expressed anger that in the early 1960s young blacks seemed to lose interest in his style of blues to embrace the newer styles of soul and rhythm and blues (outgrowths of gospel music), and that it was white youngsters who displayed the most affinity for what he did. Waters often credited the Rolling Stones with reviving his career in the 1960s and with exposing white audiences to his music for the first time.

There's much truth in that assessment. But at the same time, an impossibly sturdy cultural barrier had been erected to contain the music and art of African-Americans. It wasn't until the 1970s that music by black artists was programmed extensively on radio stations outside of black neighborhoods. The flap during the 1980s about MTV's reluctance to air videos by black performers is reminiscent of radio's earlier aversion to airing black musicians.

Jazz, Delta blues, Chicago blues, rhythm and blues, soul, and gospel all first appeared on what were called "race records," considered taboo for "mainstream" radio for a long time. Their content was sneeringly dismissed by programmers and many listeners as "nigger music." It wasn't until the mid-1950s—when snake-hipped white performers, most of them young, rural southerners, began recording adaptations of the music they'd grown up with—that "nigger music" became acceptable in the larger culture. Even then it was a slow, often acrimonious process. Those adaptations, of course, came to be known as rock and roll—a "revolutionary" style whose foundation actually stretched back more than half a century to the tarpaper shacks, shimmering fields of cotton, and lonely plantation crossroads of the Mississippi Delta.

A dedicated fan of Muddy Waters, Texas guitarist Johnny Winter (left) cajoled the blues legend back into the recording studio in 1976 for a four-album collaboration with some of the original Headhunters.

Bibliography

Albertson, Chris. Liner notes, *Bessie Smith: The Complete Recordings*, Vol. 1. New York: Columbia Records, 1992.

Calt, Stephen, and Gail Wardlow. *King of the Delta Blues: The Life And Music of Charlie Patton*. Newton, N.J.: Rock Chapel Press, 1988.

Charters, Samuel Barclay. *Bluesmen: The Blues Makers*. New York: Da Capo Press, 1991.

Guralnick, Peter. *The Listener's Guide to the Blues*. Facts on File, 1982.

Hadlock, Richard. *Jazz Masters of the 20's*. New York: Macmillan, 1965.

LaVere, Stephen C. Liner notes, *Robert Johnson: The Complete Recordings*. New York: Columbia Records, 1991.

Marsh, Dave, and John Swenson, eds. *The Rolling Stone Record Guide*. New York: Random House/Rolling Stone Press, 1979.

Obrecht, James, ed. *Blues Guitar: The Men Who Made the Music* (from the pages of *Guitar Player* magazine). Milwaukee: GPI Books, 1990.

Palmer, Robert. *Deep Blues*. New York: Viking Press, 1981.

Sallis, James. *The Guitar Players*. New York: Quill, 1982.

Suggested Reading

Cone, James H. *The Spirituals and the Blues: An Interpretation*. Maryknoll, N.Y.: Orbis Books, 1991.

Cook, Bruce. *Listen to the Blues*. New York: Charles Scribner's Sons, 1973.

Dixon, Willie, and Don Snowden. *I Am the Blues: The Willie Dixon Story*. London: Quartet Books, 1989.

Fahey, John Aloysius. *Charley Patton*. London: Studio Vista, 1970.

Finn, Julio. *The Bluesman: The Musical Heritage of Black Men and Women in the Americas*. London: Quartet Books, 1986.

Garon, Paul and Beth. *Woman With Guitar: Memphis Minnie's Blues*. New York: Da Capo Press, 1992.

Guralnick, Peter. *Feel Like Going Home: Portraits in Blues and Rock 'n' Roll*. New York: Penguin Book USA, 1992.

————. *Searching for Robert Johnson*. New York: Dutton, 1989.

Harris, Sheldon. *Blues Who's Who: A Biographical Dictionary of Blues Singers*. New Rochelle, N.Y.: Arlington House, 1979.

Harrison, Daphne Duval. *Black Pearls: Blues Queens Of The 1920's*. Rutgers, N.J.: Rutgers University Press, 1988.

Kozinn, Allan; Pete Welding; Dan Forte; and Gene Santoro. *The Guitar: The History, The Music, The Players*. New York: Quill, 1984.

Marcus, Greil. *Mystery Train*. New York: Dutton, 1975.

Neff, Robert, and Anthony Connor. *Blues*. Boston: D.R. Godine, 1975.

Oliver, Paul. *The Story of the Blues*. Philadelphia: Chilton Book Co., 1969.

Rowe, Mike. *Chicago Breakdown*. New York: Drake Publishers, 1975.

Ruppli, Michel. *The Chess Labels: A Discography*. Westport, Conn.: Greenwood Press, 1983.

Russell, Tony. *Blacks, Whites, and Blues*. New York: Stein and Day, 1970.

Sallis, James. *The Guitar Players*. New York: Quill, 1982.

Stewart-Baxter, Derrick. *Ma Rainey and the Classic Blues Singers*. New York: Stein and Day, 1970.

Tirro, Frank. *Jazz: A History*. New York: Norton, 1977.

Titon, Jeff and Todd. *Early Downhome Blues: A Musical and Cultural Analysis*. Champlaign, Ill.: University of Illinois Press, 1977.

Vulliamy, Graham. *Jazz & Blues*. London: Routledge & Kegan Paul, 1982.

Welding, Pete, and Toby Byron. *Bluesland: Portraits of Twelve Major American Blues Masters*. New York: Dutton, 1991.

Wolfe, Charles K., and Kip Lornell. *The Life and Legend of Leadbelly*. New York: Harper Collins, 1992.

Suggested Listening

Broonzy, Big Bill. *Good Time Tonight*. Sony/CBS.

Dixon, Willie. *The Willie Dixon Chess Box*. Chess.

Fuller, Blind Boy. *East Coast Piedmont Style*. Sony/CBS.

Hooker, John Lee. *Boogie Chillen*. Charly.

House, Son. *Death Letter*. Edsel

Howlin' Wolf. *The Howlin' Wolf Chess Box*. Chess.

————. *The Rockin' Chair Album*. Chess.

Hurt, Mississippi John. *The Immortal Mississippi John Hurt*. Vanguard.

James, Elmore. *Shake Your Moneymaker*. Charly.

James, Skip. *Today!* Vanguard.

Jefferson, Blind Lemon. *King of the Country Blues*. Yazoo.

Johnson, Blind Willie. *The Complete Recordings*. Sony/CBS.

Johnson, Lonnie. *Steppin' on the Blues*. Sony/CBS.

Johnson, Robert. *The Complete Recordings*. Sony/CBS.

Leadbelly. *Huddie Ledbetter's Best*. Capitol.

Little Walter. *The Best of Little Walter,* Vols. I & II. Chess.

Memphis Minnie. *Hoodoo Lady*. Sony/CBS.

Muddy Waters. *The Best of Muddy Waters*. Chess.

————. *The Muddy Waters Chess Box*. Chess.

Patton, Charley. *Founder of the Delta Blues*. Yazoo.

Rogers, Jimmy. *Left Me with a Broken Heart*. Chess.

Smith, Bessie. *The Complete Recordings*. Sony/CBS.

Tampa Red. *The Guitar Wizard*. Blues Classics.

White, Booker T. Washington "Bukka." *Legacy of the Blues*. Takoma.

Williamson, John Lee "Sonny Boy." *Throw a Boogie Woogie*. RCA.

Williamson, Sonny Boy (Rice Miller). *Down & Out Blues*. Chess.

Photography Credits

Index